MONET

By: ALBERTO MARTINI

AVENEL BOOKS
NEW YORK

First U.S. Edition published 1978 by Avenel Books
distributed by Crown Publishers Inc.
Printed in Italy by Fabbri Editori, Milan.
a b c d e f g h i

Library of Congress Cataloging in Publication Data
Monet, Claude, 1840-1926.
Monet.
Translation of Claude Monet.
1. Monet, Claude, 1840-1926. I. Martini, Alberto.
ND553.M7A4 1978a 759.4 78-59682
ISBN 0-517-24954-5

Claude-Oscar Monet was born in Paris on November 14, 1840. He was the oldest son of a grocery store owner, who five years after Claude's birth moved with his family to Le Havre. In this city Monet began his studies and showed an early talent for art. From 1856 to 1858 he studied drawing under a certain F.J. Ochard. His first passion was for caricature and he was very successful at it. Then, under the guidance of the landscape painter Eugène Boudin, his first real master, he came to love painting outdoors, en plein air.

In 1859 he went to Paris and spent all his time at the Salon, where he was attracted to the works of Daubigny and particularly to Troyon, from whom he received encouragement, thanks to a letter of introduction by Boudin. Although he was a student at the Académie he did not attend the courses given there. Instead, against everyone's advice he worked mostly on his own. He did attend Charles Jacques's studio as well as the free courses at the Académie Suisse, where he met Pissarro.

Familiarizing himself with Delacroix's work and in discussions at the Brasserie des Martyrs, he enriched his cultural patrimony. In all, he learned more from his artistic experience than from any academic teaching. In the fall of 1860 he was called into the French army and went to Algeria with the African Chasseurs. Having fallen ill with anemia there, he returned to Le Havre in 1862 to recuperate. His family finally agreed to pay the tax to free him from serving in the army. In exchange he promised to study with a serious painter. This period at Le Havre was a particularly happy one for the young painter as he roamed the countryside and seashore to paint the Normandy landscape. During these excursions he was often in the company of Boudin or Jongkind. In the fall, in Paris, he entered Gleyre's studio, where he met Bazille, Renoir, and Sisley—painters with whom he would maintain strong bonds of friendship for the rest of his life. The most important encounters during this period were with Manet, whose paintings he had seen in a show in 1863, and, in the following year, after Gleyre's atelier was closed, with the paintings of Courbet. Endlessly, Monet argued with his family, who did not approve of his independent and rebellious nature and refused to support him. To make ends meet, he had to work ceaselessly outdoors—in the Forest of Fontainebleau, along the banks of the Seine, and in Normandy. The only help he received was from Courbet, and especially from the devoted Bazille, his painter friends.

In 1866, after having had modest success at the Salon with a full-length portrait of Camille Doncieux, he again began receiving financial support from his family, but not for very long. Discovering that he was living with Camille, they insisted he leave her, even though she was at that moment giving birth to a boy, Jean, with only Bazille to assist in the birth. Penniless, desperate, Monet was living with an aunt at Sainte-Adresse and could not leave. These difficult times prevented him from painting with any regularity. He was always on the move, like a vagabond, drifting between Paris and Normandy, escaping from his creditors, or hoping to obtain the money which a friend or an occasional collector had promised. In spite of all these adverse circumstances, he was able to create beautiful paintings. He married Camille in 1870, and they fled to London that same year because of the Franco-Prussian war. His friend Bazille died a year later during that war. After a trip to Belgium, he returned to Paris at the end of 1871 and rented a small house in Argenteuil on the banks of the Seine. He was no longer in a state of despondency, which in the previous years had driven him to attempt suicide, but the times were still fraught with financial difficulties for him. He was, however, able to paint with some regularity because of the help he received from the art dealer Durand-Ruel, the only person who believed in Monet and his friends Renoir, Sisley, Pissarro and Cezanne. It was with these painters, as well as with Degas and Morisot, that he organized the first group show, ironically baptized "Impressionists," a name derived from a Monet painting, Impression: The Rising Sun. *Almost no one in 1874 believed that these young painters were serious. The visitors at Nadar's studio were scandalized; they thought, at best, it was no more than an absurd and ridiculous joke. But a couple of paintings were sold, and a small number of critics had the courage to support the Impressionists publicly. These shows were organized again in 1876, 1877, 1880, 1881, 1882 and 1886. Monet, however, did not participate in the fifth, sixth and eighth exhibitions, for he disagreed with some of the tendencies as well as with some of the sponsors. In the beginning of 1878, Monet left Argenteuil and moved to Vétheuil. Camille was weak and sick. Her health was undermined after the birth of her second son, Michel, and in September 1879, she died. Monet continued his life as a hunter in search of "impressions." Poissy, Varengeville, Dieppe, Pourville and Etretat were his favorite places.*

He finally settled in Giverny. From there he traveled a couple of times to the South of France, alone or in the company of Renoir. In the meantime, his financial situation began showing signs of improvement, though he had to support the now bankrupt Hoschédé family, who had previously been his patrons. His shows at the Durand-Ruel and at the Petit galleries met with both critical and financial success, and in 1880, he was at last able to buy the house in Giverny. Two years later he married Mme Hoschédé. He traveled less now, though he still made occasional trips to Normandy, a trip to Norway in 1895, a few visits to London (in 1889, 1900, 1901 and 1904), a short stay in Madrid to see the paintings of Velasquez in 1904 and two brief visits to Venice in 1908 and 1909.

Most of Monet's time was now occupied in caring for his garden and pond, taking particular pains with the plants and the flowers that he painted unceasingly. He was indifferent to his fame as the major living French artist and to the glory that he had attained with so much work at such a high price. He was also indifferent to the praises and honors that were bestowed upon him by other painters, writers and politicians. The person closest to Monet from this last group was the proud Georges Clémenceau. Monet never felt he had succeeded, and he strove to surpass everything he had achieved before. He agonized over the daily problem of trying to reach the limits of his perception.

A painful eye disease did not curb his enthusiasm, and he continued to work on his last paintings until his death in his house in Giverny on the 5th of December 1926.

A new vision of reality revealed by the eye of the most penetrating Impressionist painter.

Asters—Private collection.

Claude Monet's name is intimately connected with the history of Impressionism, its formation, its development, its conclusions. This is the supreme mark of his artistic importance. The Impressionist movement gloriously completed the researches of Naturalism and laid the groundwork for modern art. Monet was the first and foremost contributor to the birth of Impressionism and to the new manner of expressing a vision, where reality was interpreted in ways never before imagined—fresh, airy, harmonious, where colors dazzled in all of their solar intensity, where nature was discovered in joyous vibrating life and in changing skies. "I paint as a bird sings," Monet told his friend Geoffroy, and with these candid words he described the natural spontaneity of his work. Monet's song revolutionized the course of modern painting. He represents the turning point from what was painted before him to what came after him. Before Monet, even the painters who were close to Impressionism painted the shadows in neutral tones. Their paintings were laid out in zones of light and dark and were often executed in patches. The atmosphere and the time of the day were painted with a balance that made everything look immobile. Light was considered a phenomenon which revealed the miraculous beauty and unity of form. After Monet's creative work, even shadows were given color, and forms were now defined by a live vibrating light. Painting became a fragmented image that found its place within the whole. This natural image was represented in all its freedom and mobility.

Next to Monet even the paintings of Delacroix look far less luminous, Corot's liveliest paintings breathe the air of the studio and Manet's work stresses his own academic virtuosity. But Monet's canvases are a direct transcription of the passing moment. He used color as if it were exploding in myriad fragmented brushstrokes, bringing out the light, inundating the canvas with a solar intensity that tinges even the shadows. It was a new way of seeing and representing the world. The public at first saw only the unstructured quality of his sketches and his absurd chromatic arbitrariness. Painters were puzzled when confronted with his style, which questioned all the basic principles of painting. Even the best critics, after having praised the freshness of the "impression," complained that he left the paintings at an early unfinished stage. But this was precisely Monet's originality and strength, for the primary outline and sketches translated the immediacy of the impression and expressed the fidelity of Monet's observation beyond any conventional representation.

Every object, person or landscape lives within its own changing atmosphere and light, each color affects the next one, and upon careful observation we see that the reflection of the green foliage of trees tints clothes and faces, the same way the sky tints the water in which it is reflected. In nature there are no limited, isolated colors, and the shadows are not neutral. There are shaded areas in which colors affect each other reciprocally, varying from the sunny areas in degrees of luminosity. No one before Monet had analyzed this optical phenomenon with such awareness and subtlety; no one had had the courage to take into consideration that, at a distance, woods or houses become almost indistinguishable masses. Of course, understanding and experience teach us that some tree branches grow closer together and some further apart and that every house is different in a thousand details, but visually this is not the case. Monet refused to paint what people thought they knew of things—he painted what he saw. In order to obtain these results, which were not programmed but derived from his own temperament and sensibility, Monet found himself obliged to invent a new representational language, a new style; solutions offered by traditional painting were completely inadequate. Drawing, chiaroscuro, linear perspective, blotches, tones and values could no longer serve his needs. He created a technique of painting with separated brushstrokes, dashes, commas, where color dazzled with light, where the atmosphere moved and space vibrated with light. Each brushstroke was clearly separated from the next one. There were no overlaps or shadings. They were no longer needed, for if the observation of the painter was correct, the image would compose itself naturally in the eye of the observer. In this lay Monet's intelligence. He felt that to go forward in art it would be necessary to use the sensory and rational experiences of the viewer, compelling him to put into the work his own understanding and perceptions as well as his interpretation. In fact, the development of Monet's art, from his first timid experiments with landscapes to the daring representations of the water-lilies series, almost dissolved within the atmosphere and at the threshold of losing all recognizable form, was the result of the study of light and its phenomena. Monet realized that he had increased the visual

The Garden at Giverny—Private collection.

capacity of those who followed him and understood his work. He had to struggle in order to gain acceptance for his new vision, at times in precarious and even tragic financial situations, but toward the end of the century he won the understanding and support of a good number of critics and collectors, who encouraged him to be even more daring. He now had the proof that his new technique was not merely bizzare and gratuitous, but could be useful in helping others to increase their understanding of reality. Monet focused his interests predominantly on the problems of vision and representation. While this forced him to bold and previously unattempted artistic expression, it also generated criticism and interpretive distortions. He was often considered just a mechanical eye, recording faithfully and scientifically all visual impressions. Cezanne said of him, "Monet is only an eye, but my God, what an eye!".

Monet was considered an intellectual revolutionary, a skillful decorator who showed his limits in his late paintings, which were splendid failures. These criticisms were unjust not only to the brilliance of the artist, but also to his lyrical and delicate sensibility, which expressed an authentic grace and a natural gentleness. Monet was the first to realize the instinctive union of the eye and the heart, of the observation of reality and its lyrical transformation, which was the basic principle of Impressionism. He did so with a passion and fidelity for his own emotional and stylistic reasons, which were characterized by a total coherence, a necessary coherence. When one speaks of "impression," and in Monet's case it happens frequently, one is referring not only to a visual phenomenon, but also to the artist's own emotions. We see only what we choose to see, what we like to see. Monet liked fresh air, sunlight—nature. He celebrated his love of nature with the freshness and the instinctive joy of someone who felt rewarded, of someone who was exalted in the face of beauty. His eyes were the first to discover and reveal it, his soul was the first to feel its vibration and splendor.

The course of Monet's life was steady and controlled, without upheavals or dispersion. After his first experiences in the field of caricature he had the good fortune to meet Eugène Boudin, who convinced him to put his easel outdoors and paint there. Boudin was no great painter; his views were conventional, but he was able to teach his young student the infinite possibilities of on-site painting and the beauty of nature under real light. He taught Monet, "everything which is painted directly in its own surroundings appears forceful; it carries a strength, a vitality in the touch that cannot be found in the studio." Monet treasured this knowledge all his life. Boudin was also aware that he could not give his student much more than his love for landscape, and he wisely encouraged Monet to go to Paris, for it was only in an atmosphere alive with discussion and ferment that an artist can grow.

In 1859, at the age of nineteen, Monet arrived in Paris, the artistic capital of Europe, already firmly decided in the direction he would follow. Monet was sure of himself. He took sides with the landscape painters even more than with Corot and Troyon, whom he appreciated as painters. But he felt close to Daubigny. It did not matter to him that this painter was criticized by those who appreciated the landscape painters, or that such a subtle and intelligent critic as Théophile Gautier commented with bitterness upon Daubigny's paintings: "They show us only juxtaposed blotches of color." In this artistic climate, Monet made his choices. How important was it for Monet to follow Troyon's advice and visit the studio of such a traditional painter as Couture? What weight could he give to his family's urging that he study in the studio of a serious painter? He understood that academic teaching dimmed the light of nature and cooled the warmth of life, that drawing and chiaroscuro exercises deadened the immediate impression. All of this was enough to make him reject academic discipline. He hated the Academie so much that when faced with the choice given to him by his parents between studying at the Académie and enrolling in the army, he chose to leave for Algeria, with the regiment of African Chasseurs. It was to be a short stay. Monet fell ill at the beginning of 1862 and had to return to his family. He then had to promise them that he would attend the painting courses in Gleyre's atelier regularly.

Before he returned to Paris, Monet met the painter Jongkind, who confirmed his feelings about art. It was a fortunate encounter because this restless Dutch painter was perhaps the most experimental artist of the avant-garde. Jongkind was trying to develop a language which would allow painters to represent the variations of light and of the atmosphere. His nervous brushstrokes undoubtedly convinced Monet to elaborate on the techniques that Boudin and Daubigny had shown him, and he now had the courage to apply them with new strength.

During the years of enforced study in Gleyre's atelier, Monet did not attend classes regularly, preferring to work outdoors whenever he could. Often he and other young students went to Chailly, in the Forest of Fontainebleau, a place dear to the painters of The Barbizon landscape school whom they particularly admired. Among Monet's friends were Bazille, who was not yet sure of himself and was still tied to academic conventions; Renoir, who was attracted to the pictorial vigor of Courbet; and Sisley who still remained under Corot's influence. Monet was the only one who already had the experience of painting outdoors under the guidance of Boudin and Jongkind. He was the only one with the uncompromising rigor of an initiate, who fought for a modern naturalism where his vision would not be clouded by prejudices and ambiguous traditions. From then on he assumed the leadership of this new artistic movement.

Monet's artistry developed steadily. When he reached a new point, he immediately tried to go beyond it, to gain new ground with an insistence which was to characterize him all his life. It was a passionate investigation of the world and its representation. His creative period extended over a period of a little less than seventy years; it can be viewed as an unwavering line, because his eyes, in spite of his last illness, remained eternally youthful. He was constantly amazed by the spectacle of the world, the vitality of nature in the changing light of the sun. For it is the sun that helps plants and flowers to grow—the plants and flowers he loved.

In 1864, Monet became more specifically concerned with areas of juxtaposed colors, particularly in the landscape paintings that he made along the banks of the Seine and in the countryside around Honfleur. Monet's luminous sensibility was at this point circumscribed within the conventional scheme of Courbet's ideas, a certain expansion of composition and a preestablished use of light and shadow.

The year 1865 marks the maturation of Monet's ideas and of his vision. In his large canvas, *Le Déjeûner sur l'Herbe,* he used one of Manet's themes, but freed it from any traditional tie by treating it with fragmented brushstrokes. Thus he created a vibrating light which rendered a greater sense of reality. The treatment of figures within a landscape was interpreted with a vivacious brushwork and color unknown even to Courbet and Manet. Courbet's advice and suggestions diverted Monet from his own ends, preoccupied him with problems which were not his, to the point of compromising his already outstanding work. Monet's huge *Déjeûner sur l'Herbe* was rolled up in a corner, and part of the canvas rotted. Only two fragments of this enormous composition remain, one in the Musée du Louvre and one in the Eknayan Collection, Paris. A smaller painting is in the Pushkin Museum, Moscow, and a study for the left side of the painting is in the Molyneux collection, Paris. The Russian sketch, dated 1866, is the most luminous and is the lightest in feeling, executed with a more airy and fluttering touch than the two large fragments. It was probably a preparatory work for the larger painting. It is more faithful to the impression, because it was probably painted on the spot, though signed and dated the following year.

This painting and *Women in the Garden* (Musee du Louvre, Paris) of 1866-67, along with the landscapes he painted in the same years, in Honfleur and in Paris, are miracles of sensibility and observation. They are considered the beginning of a new stage of Impressionism. Between Monet and nature there were no longer any intellectual screens. When Renoir took him to the Louvre to study the masters, Monet preferred to look out the window and sketch his impressions of nature. Through his eyes and through his vision, a relationship suddenly appeared which connected the artist's awareness to the external world. At this point, nothing else mattered for him.

His friends followed in his path, aroused by his enthusiasm and by the originality of his discovery, sharing the anguishes of his researches and the joy of his achievements. Those most influenced

Two Fishermen—Cambridge, Fogg Art Museum.

were Renoir and Sisley, who quickly overcame Courbet's and Corot's respective influences, and Pissarro, once liberated from Millet's ascendancy. Bazille, who died young, had remained attached to Manet's broad style, while Cézanne used a new pictorial language to emerge from the romantic works of his youth. These were the Impressionists. With canvases, easels and boxes of colors in hand they searched the banks of the Seine for the themes closest to their sensibilities and temperaments—clumps of flowers, the glow of light, reflections on the water, the quivering of foliage, running clouds, mist and smoke. These painters, and especially Monet, were attracted to the changing and airy aspects of nature. In their enthusiasm they wanted to show how the eye could catch the impression of a fleeting moment, how this impression could be painted on canvas without betraying its mobility and its freshness. From about 1870 to 1884 the Impressionists worked more or less as a group, even joined by the proud Manet. Then their paths separated, and each painter developed his own personal style. Monet contributed the most to the creation of a new theory translated into a new artistic language. He had no doubts. For him this was the only truth, the truth he felt inside himself. In this light, the development of Monet's art is nothing more than the ripening of these new possibilities of expression. He applied his flitting, caressing touch to limited areas of the canvas, corresponding to the natural themes. Later, this technique became dominant in his painting. At certain times of the day, and in some places, particularly along the cliffs of Normandy, reality seemed to be made up of vibrating light, and Monet's hands traced minute, comma-like brushstrokes which brought to life his visual impressions. One can perceive the remote influence of Japanese prints in the structure of his compositions, as well as in his bold aerial perspectives and in the synthesis of elements in his own visual field. Monet refused to resolve the problem of the representation of light by a synthesis of the different areas of colors. He preferred an elaborate cross-rhythmed brushstroke which created a special luminous effect. By this method, Monet discovered a new and beautiful pictorial texture as well as a new organic vitality.

And this must be understood as part of the visual image which is stimulated by natural observation, and not as an abstract language in itself.

Forms began dissolving in the airy vibrations of Monet's brushstrokes, almost suspended in luminosity. Monet felt that he had departed from the truth of nature, and that he had allowed himself to be guided towards an impossible goal. In his search for light, he had lost contact with reality. He did not give up his field of research; he limited it. He no longer "foraged all over France like a hunter in search of impressions," as Guy de Maupassant said, but concentrated on the untiring observation of a single subject, seen under different light at different times of the day and in different seasons. This is how he created his famous series of paintings, those of 1891, depicting haystacks and poplars, and the best known, those of 1894, dedicated to the Cathedral of Rouen. Monet complained that he no longer had his youthful readiness to grasp instantaneous impressions; he tormented himself for not being able to follow the sun in its own course through the sky. He was desperate because he was unable to finish a painting and was forced to repaint it in order to come closer to his perception of reality. In effect, the way he saw the visible world was changing.

Under the influence of the new cultural climate of post-Impressionism, which was characterized by the research of symbolic equivalences between form and inner being, Monet also began to pay attention to the role of imagination in the representation of nature. The instinctive relation between eye and feeling, between a faithful representation of reality and the artist's lyrical transformation of this same reality was the fundamental characteristic of Impressionism. This can be seen in the paintings Monet made in London and Venice, as well as in the great series of paintings showing his own garden and pond in Giverny, the *Water Lilies.* These paintings occupied Monet's last years. Water lilies gave life to the skies and waters, reflecting the vitality of nature, its perpetual growth, the variations in its light as well as in its mournful extinction. In nature as Monet painted it was reflected a soul which vibrated with compassion in front of a growing plant and a flower in full bloom, but which was at times veiled in a melancholic mood, at others inflamed with passion or shaken by a desperate agitation. Monet's furious imagination was exalted in these great canvases and expressed itself in a thickly colored impasto. With the *Water Lily* series, the creative stream of the artist came to an end, and thus, as Clemenceau said, closed the "eye of a precursor," who "had rendered with a greater penetration . . . our perception of the universe."

Index of the illustrations

I - Shipyard near Honfleur - Private collection - *This is one of the first important paintings made by Monet in 1864, during a period of intense formative experiences in Normandy with his painter friends Jongkind, Boudin, and Courbet. In this painting his sensitivity to light is still tied to traditional concepts, and the color is conventional.*

II - Camille, or the Woman in the Green Dress - Bremen, Kunsthalle - *With this portrait of his friend Camille Doncieux, Monet won a prize at the Salon of 1866, obtaining his first important critical and public success. The delicate play of the light among the folds of the dress captured in the liveliness of the moment seems to bring life to the figure.*

III - Déjeuner sur l'herbe - (detail of a fragment) - Paris, Musée du Louvre - *This painting with its life-size figures marks an important stage in the impressionist evolution of Monet. It was begun at Chailly on August 1865. Monet spent a great deal of time in working out the theme, making numerous studies, for he feared that he would lose the freshness of the composition on the large canvas.*

IV - The Church of St. Germain l'Auxerrois in Paris - West Berlin, Charlottenburg, Nationalgalerie - *It is noteworthy that this work of 1866 was painted in the Louvre. Rather than copy the paintings of the masters, Monet preferred to look out of the museum's windows to study the play of light and color in the street outside.*

V - Garden of the Infante - Oberlin, Ohio, Allen Memorial Art Museum, Oberlin College - *This painting of 1867 is part of those views of Paris that Monet made in the spring of that year, affirming his inclination to work outdoors.*

VI - Jean Monet in His Crib - Private collection - *The first son that Monet had with Camille Doncieux was born on August 8, 1867. The artist depicted his son in the crib, attentively watched by the seated woman. A blueish light creates an intimacy expressive of the love that Monet felt within him.*

VII - Women in a Garden - Paris, Musée du Louvre - *Monet begen this painting in 1866 during his stay at Ville d'Avray; he finished the work during the following year. Much of it was painted outdoors, and as the canvas was very large it had to be lowered into a small ditch while Monet painted the upper part. The model for the four figures was his wife Camille.*

VIII-IX - The Grenouillère - New York, The Metropolitan Museum of Art, Bequest of Mrs. O. Havemeyer, 1929 - *This work of 1869 testifies to the long friendship and the creativity he shared with Renoir. With its rapid brushstrokes it depicts one of the landscapes preferred by Monet and the other impressionist painters.*

X - The Breakwater at Le Havre - Private collection - *At the International Maritime Exposition of Le Havre of 1868, Monet won a medal for the freshness of his paintings depicting various views of the region. Monet was fascinated by the ceaseless movement of the sea and the boats, as well as by the endlessly varied reflections on the water and in the sky.*

XI - The Entrance of the Port of Honfleur - Los Angeles, The Norton Simon Foundation - *Monet painted this work in 1867 during a period that was very difficult economically. But it was also a period of intense artistic activity. The rapid rhythm of the brushstrokes and the intense vibration of the light make this an impressionistic work.*

XII - The Voorzaan near Zaandam - Private collection - *At the outbreak of the war in 1870 Monet had fled to London. The following year he went to Holland with his family. There, on the Voorzaan River, he recaptured the magic of nature, sparkling with light and modulated in the infinite delicacy of the tones on his canvases.*

XIII - Windmill near Zaandam - Private collection - *Monet made several paintings, as well as a drawing, of this subject when he had already left Holland. This painting of 1882, that was certainly begun the year before, perfectly expresses the flat Dutch landscape.*

XIV - Impression: Sunrise - Paris, Musée Marmottan - *After the show of the independent artists at Nadar's studio in 1874, this painting of 1872 was to become the symbol of that group of painters and would also provide the name for the movement. It synthesizes Monet's style: reality assumes the infinite possibilities of the image that the artist's personal intuition can provide.*

XV - The Boat-Studio - Otterlo, Kröller-Müller Stichting - *In 1874 Monet depicted the boat on which he passed entire days painting, as Daubigny had done before him, moving along the Seine River searching for images to transfer to canvas. The reflections on the water and the intense vibrations of the light made his boat-studio an ideal observation point.*

XVI - Regatta at Argenteuil - Paris, Musée du Louvre - *In this painting of 1874, one can see how Monet, in order to represent nature as it appears to his sensitive eye, employs the division of color tones with short and divided brushstrokes, juxtaposing the complementary colors that perfectly reveal the minutest variations of the light.*

XVII - Regatta at Argenteuil - Paris, Musée du Louvre - *Water was always an ideal subject for Monet's paintings. He was always drawn to certain parts of the Seine, and in 1872 he moved to Argenteuil, whose beautiful landscape was to become an inexhaustible source of inspiration for all the impressionist painters.*

XVIII - Regatta at Sainte-Adresse - New York, The Metropolitan Museum of Art, Bequest of William Church Osborn, 1951 - *During the course of his artistic evolution, Monet rarely painted the human figure. It is present in this work of 1867, but his interest in nature progressively attracted more and more of his attention.*

XIX - Windmill in Amsterdam - Private collection - *Monet returned for a brief visit to Holland in 1874, and this time he painted the streets, the canals, and the windmills of Amsterdam. With an ever more refined impressionistic technique he transcribed his sensations with thick brushstrokes that became shorter and more colored.*

XX - Monet's House at Argenteuil - Private collection - *In his full artistic maturity Monet was able to emphasize and boldly breakdown pure colors, not only in order to bring them out, but to express the vibrations of the light so that he could give form to his sensations. In this painting of 1876 his simple house has been transformed by the vibrations of the light.*

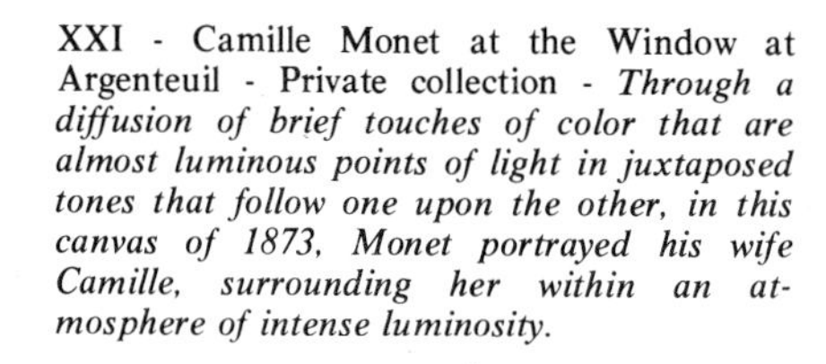

XXI - Camille Monet at the Window at Argenteuil - Private collection - *Through a diffusion of brief touches of color that are almost luminous points of light in juxtaposed tones that follow one upon the other, in this canvas of 1873, Monet portrayed his wife Camille, surrounding her within an atmosphere of intense luminosity.*

XXII - The Artist's Family in the Garden of Argenteuil - Private collection - *The brilliance of Monet's art consists in his having intuited that bright light nullifies color so that, in his landscapes, the rays of the reflecting sun dissolve into pure luminosity, while the shadows come to life due to the intense tones of color.*

XXIII - Rosebushes in Hoschedé's Garden at Montgeron - Private collection - *The main subject of the investigation of the impressionists was not to depict colors and objects, but to represent the particular suggestions that such colors and objects assumed due to the light and its endless variations.*

XXIV-XXV - Poppies near Argenteuil - Private collection - *The countryside around Argenteuil was of constant inspiration for Monet. He painted many works in this region in 1875 and 1876, when he was in his full impressionistic maturity. He enveloped every subject within the vibration of the light, blending figures with nature.*

XXVI - The Banks of the Seine at Courbevoie - Paris, Musée Marmottan - *When Monet's difficult economic situation compelled him to leave Argenteuil in 1878 and settle in the outskirts of Paris, he seemed to have rediscovered the enchantment of the Seine, with its white houses along the banks and its rows of poplar trees.*

XXVII - Appletrees at Vétheuil - Private collection - *After several months near Paris at the end of 1878, Monet painted the small country towns such as the one where he lived, with its hills and vegetation that provided him with the subjects to enflame his imagination.*

XXVIII-XXIX - The Station of St. Lazare - Paris, Musée du Louvre - *In this painting of 1877 that represent a variation in the pictorial research of Monet, he employed a new and extremely suggestive theme for a painter who perceived the world through the vibrations of the atmosphere: the smoke and the vapor of the locomotive.*

XXX - The Road of Vétheuil in Winter - Göteborg, Konstmuseum - *Painted in 1879, the year of Camille's death, this work does not have an unusual theme for Monet who confronts the subject with a new technical rigor and structure, and with a brushwork that has become longer and more precise.*

XXXI - Lavacourt - Private collection - *It was a view of Lavacourt, the small town near Vétheuil that Monet depicted several times in 1878 and 1879, that brought him recognition and success in 1880 when it was accepted and displayed at the Salon. It was highly praised in several reviews, and especially in an article by Emile Zola.*

XXXII - The Railroad Bridge at Argenteuil - Paris, Musée du Louvre - *For the impressionists who always sought the countryside near the city, the many trains that passed through the outskirts of Paris were a familiar sight. Monet must have been particularly struck by the light filtering through the steam and the soot of the locomotive.*

XXXIII - Rue St. Denis, National Holiday of June 30, 1878 - Rouen, Musée des Beaux-Arts - *The street filled with the joyous movement of the crowd and the flags, which light up the whole scene with color, is captured by Monet with an immediacy that makes this painting one of the landmarks of impressionism.*

XXXIV - Vétheuil in the Summer - New York, The Metropolitan Museum of Art, Bequest of William Church Osborn - *In 1880, when this painting was made, Monet, in complete control of his impressionistic technique, seemed to have found a certain difficulty in attaining spontaneity in his impressions, and his sureness comes close to a type of preciousness.*

XXXV - Sunset at Lavacourt - Paris, Musée du Petit Palais - *At the end of the 1880s, when this painting was completed, began a crisis within the impressionist movement that resulted in the individual members of the group seeking to follow their own paths, even if they remained bound to the common ideal of the liberty of expression.*

XXXVI - The Thaw - Private collection - *The thaw on the Seine, after the terribly cold winter of 1879-80, made an enormous impression on Monet, who made several versions of this scene directly from nature, and repeated it once more a year later when he left Vétheuil.*

XXXVII - The Spring - Lyons, Musée des Beaux-Arts - *Though this work is dated 1882 it was painted in 1880 when Monet still lived at Vétheuil, where it seemed that he had found the ideal place to cultivate the myth of the open-air painter.*

XXXVIII - The Sea Seen from the Cliffs near Fécamp - Private collection - *Painted during one of his stays in Normandy, which were to be repeated frequently during the following years, this painting of 1881, with its unusually high horizon-line, reflects an original solution for the composition of the work.*

XXXIX - The Sea at Varengeville - Private collection - *The crisis that Monet underwent during this period is described in the letters he wrote from Pourville-Varengeville, where he spent the spring of 1882. Probably feeling the need for new inspiration and another method of expression, he said that he was dissatisfied with his work.*

XL - Etretat, Stormy Sea - Lyons, Musée des Beaux-Arts - *His search for landscapes that could inspire his works made Monet move to Giverny in 1883, and then to the coast of Normandy on the English Channel, where the wintry atmosphere inspired him with the dramatic movement of the forces of nature.*

XLI - Under the Lemon Trees, Bordighera - Copenhagen, Ny Carlsberg Glyptotek - *At the beginning of 1884, Monet visited the Italian Riviera, stopping off at Bordighera where he was struck by the colors of the region. His desire to transfer the colors he saw to the canvas plunged him into a feverish investigation of the problem, and the studies that ensued left nothing to improvisation.*

XLII - Portrait of André Lauvray - Private collection - *This work, painted at Vétheuil in 1880, is an exception in Monet's artistic production. In fact, his portraits are very rare, and the human figure appeared mostly during his early years, to disappear almost entirely in his later paintings.*

XLIII - Self-Portrait - Private collection - *Monet painted this self-portrait in 1886 when his love for Alice Hoschedé created a very difficult situation for him. His torment and his inner suffering were reflected in this work.*

XLIV - Poplars on the Epte, Pink Effect - Private collection - *The profound personal crisis that he experienced during the last years of the 1880s, and only resolved in 1892 when he married Alice Hoschedé, provoked a profound change, but a maturation as well, in the art of Monet who by now abandoned any form of improvisation.*

XLV - Poplars on the Epte - London, Tate Gallery - *This is one of the first paintings of the series of "poplars" of 1891, and certainly one of the most direct and spontaneous. The successive versions would lead Monet to an almost merciless insistence that began to stultify the composition.*

XLVI - The Flood at Giverny - Private collection - *Having finally achieved a certain equilibrium, Monet seemed to have found, toward the end of the 19th century, the inspiration that enriched the production of his last masterpieces.*

XLVII - Fields at Giverny - Private collection - *Monet painted many landscapes at Giverny toward the end of the century. His last house inspired his most significant paintings, which he worked on with a systematic rigor.*

XLVIII - Customs House at Varongeville - Private collection - *Driven by his exasperated investigation of the phenomena of light, Monet came close in his last landscapes, such as this painting of 1897, to the current symbolist conceptions. Perhaps this was due to the literary influences that up to that time were completely foreign to him.*

XLIX - The Mediterranean near Antibes - Private collection - *The fascinating colors of the Mediterranean had suggested to Monet, in 1888, the sequence of blues, violets, and azures of this painting where the rhythm of the brushstrokes creates a continuity of contrast between the earth and the sea.*

L - The British Parliament: Effect of the Sun in the Fog - Paris, Musée du Louvre - *At the beginning of the 20th century Monet returned to those places that had inspired him in his youth. Earlier he had recorded everything according to the impression of the moment. Now he painted everything differently. In this work of 1904, the image of London is completely transformed by his imagination.*

LI - The Cathedral of Rouen in Sunlight - Paris, Musée du Louvre - *Monet's fears that his investigation of light had alienated him from nature and objects impelled him to make systematic studies of single objects. The results were a series of painting on the same theme, such as this cathedral of Rouen of 1894.*

LII - Flowers - Private collection - *In this painting of 1887, which probably depicts a corner of Monet's garden at Giverny, he once more uses the impressionistic technique with the vibrant luminosity of color that merges the form of the petals with that of the leaves.*

LIII - Morning on the Seine near Giverny - Paris, Musée du Louvre - *One can already see in this painting of 1897 the first signs of a certain sentimentalism that would draw Monet farther and farther away—especially in his last years—from a purely optical image of nature.*

LIV - Water-Lily Pond - New York, Mrs. Albert D. Lasker Coll. - *Monet had diverted a small stream that ran at the edge of his garden in order to make a small pond that would become, in its most detailed and particular aspects, the dominant theme of his last paintings.*

LV - Water-Lilies, Aquatic Landscape - Boston, Museum of Fine Arts - *While in the first painting of the pond of 1889 Monet depicted the trees in the background, the Japanese bridge, and the other aquatic plants, in this work of 1905 and in those that followed he concentrated on the water's surface, with its reflections and floating water-lilies.*

LVI-LVII - The Church of Santa Maria della Salute in Venice - Boston, Museum of Fine Arts - *A Venice immersed in a hallucinatory atmosphere of lights and colors, as in this canvas of 1908, shows how Monet had detached himself from the reality of things, by lyrically transforming his emotions.*

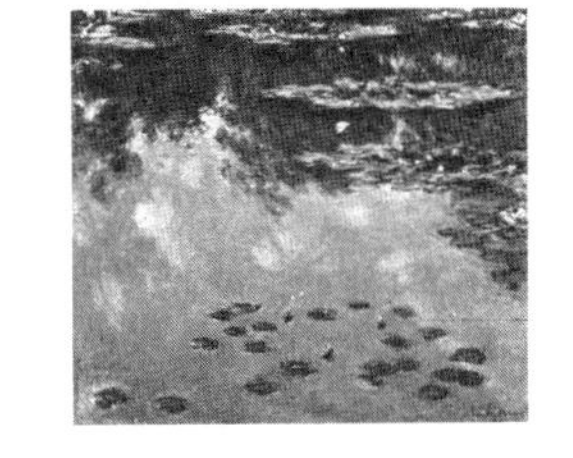

LVIII - Water-Lilies, Aquatic Landscape - Private collection - *In this version of 1906, even the hint of the edge of the pond has disappeared. There remains a mirror of water on whose surface there is a delicate play of lights and shadows that the surrounding landscape projects.*

LIX - Water-Lilies - Zürich, Kunsthaus - *Monet's emotional response to the natural settings that he portrays in the series of the water-lilies, transforming them into a festival of colors, as in this painting of 1910, or in subdued tones, mirrors the modulations of his spiritual being.*

LX - Water-Lilies, Aquatic Landscape - Private collection - *The incredible exaltation of Monet's imagination blends into a single image the sky and the water, giving to the pond's surface, in this version of 1907, a light that is worthy of the boldest romantic vision.*

LXI - Reflections on the Water - (detail) - Bagnols-sur-Cèze, Musée Léon Alègre - *The incredible technique, the complete control of his means, at times hinder the pictorial investigation of Monet who often comes close to a sense of preciousness. This painting, replete with unreal transparency, dates from 1917.*

LXII - Weeping Willow at Giverny - Private collection - *When Monet painted this weeping willow in his garden in 1918, he completely overcame the limits of his intuition and ascribed to nature the incredible hues of his passion and imagination.*

LXIII - The Garden at Giverny - Grenoble, Musée de Peinture et de Sculpture - *In the composition of the form, in the imaginative creation of colors, in the inflamed image of an unreal nature, Monet, in these last paintings, can appear as the precursor of modern painting.*

I

II

64 Claude Monet

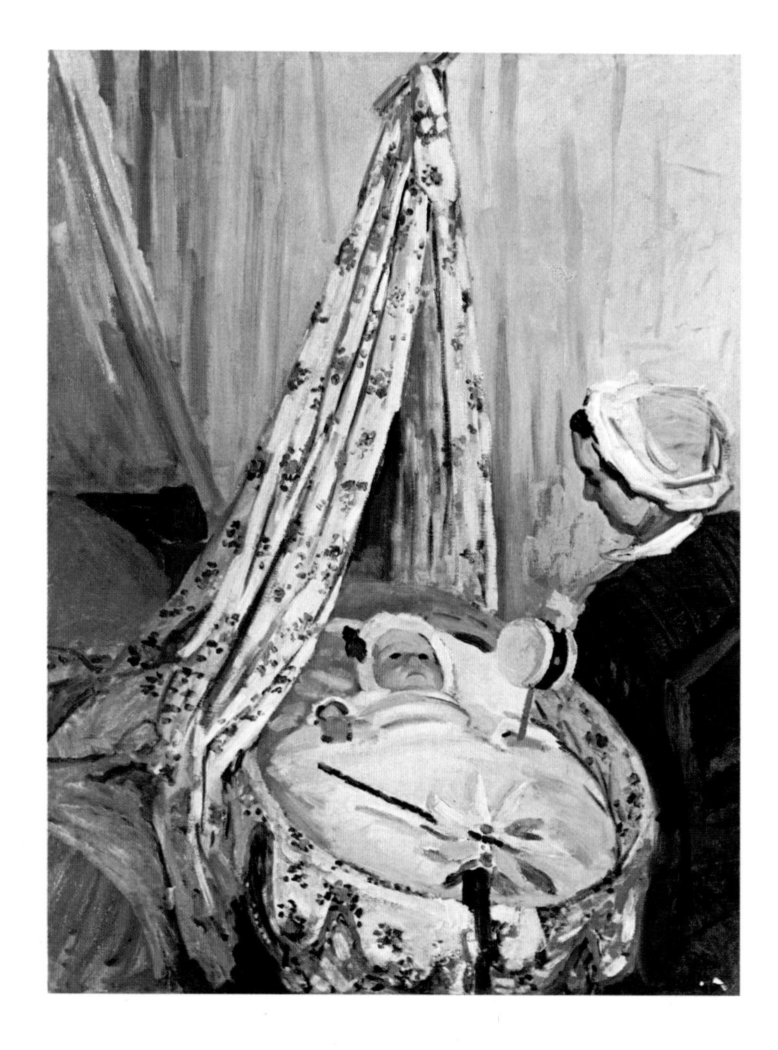

Claude Monet

VIII

IX

Claude Monet

XII

Claude Monet

Claude Monet

Claude Monet

XXIV

XXV

XXVI

XXVII

XXVIII

Claude Monet

XXXIII

XXXIV

XXXVII

XXXVIII

XLII

XLIV

XLV

XLVI

XLVIII

XLIX

L

LI

LII

LVII

LVIII

LX

LXIII

Illustrations from the Picture Archives of Fabbri Editori, Milan
Printed in June 1978, at the graphic plant of Fabbri Editori - Milan, Italy